THE KAMA~SUTRA

Erotic figures in Indian art

Presented by
Marc de Smedt

Translated by
David MacRae

MAGNA BOOKS

Credits : Bibliothèque Nationale, Paris (clichés B.N.) : 25a, b, c - 26 - 33a, b, c, c - 39a, b, - 43 a, b - 45 - 47a, b - 51 - 53a, b - 61 - 63 - 84 - 85 - 103 - 107 — Musée Guimet, Paris (clichés Réunion des Musées Nationaux) : 8 - 17 - 19 - 23 - 29 - 41 - 67 - 69 - 71 - 83 - 91 - 93 - 95 — J. L. Nou : 7 - 11 - 21 - 31 - 49 - 73 - 75 - 97 - 99 - 100 - 105 - 109 — Pizzi-Chiari/Gemini : 54 - 59 — Collection Jean Soustiel : 13 - 15 - 35 - 57 - 81 - 89 — Soustiel (clichés Tcheckov-Minosa) : 65 - 77.

We are particularly grateful to the expert, Monsieur Jean Soustiel, of Paris, for kindly authorizing us to reproduce in this volume a number of valuable documents from his collection, some of which were formerly in the collections of Joseph Soustiel and Roger Peyrefitte.

ISBN 1-85422-404-2

Printed in Italy
by G. Canale & C. S.p.A.
Borgaro T.se - Turin

1. The Kama Sutra, a sacred text

Kama Sutra—the very name is laden with erotic associations. Even those who have never read it know, or believe, that it is a treatise on the numerous postures of love described in Indian tradition. It is true that the Kama Sutra is a treatise on love written about the third century AD by a Brahman, Vatsyayana, who presented, in a condensed form, a much older body of learning already existing in the ancient sacred and esoteric texts of India and which moreover was an integral part of the ritual governing day to-day human relations.

However, in that country which gave rise to one of the great civilizations of the world, the notion of love was not confined merely to the few dozen movements and contorsions which may be observed in amorous behavior. The erotic gestures are actually nothing more than the culmination of an entire climate, of a veritable parade of love in which eyes, hands, perfumes, colors, jewels, poetry, music and an assortment of signs all convey the fine variations of feeling, and all the tonalities of desire and subtle differences of approach. Moreover, these Kama Sutra ("aphorisms of love") are profoundly embedded in Indian religion, offering, as they do, advice for the harmonious integration of the members of society, and also in the universal cosmic order which is governed by the pleiad of Hindu gods, each symbolizing a particular type of energy, a force-flow of crucial importance for the orderly working of our entire galactic system. In this sense this treatise, while not claiming to be a religious book, is closely related to the Vedas, which are among the most ancient of all sacred texts and are the basis for one of the oldest religions in the world. That religion is remarkable not only for its age but also for its wealth of interesting features: its complex cosmogony, its abundant mythology, its techniques of meditation such as the various types of yoga and pranayama (control of breathing), as well as a lordly moral code which gave rise to both brahmanism and the caste system. In India the links between the gods and men are indissoluble, since they are part of the same cosmogonic fabric: the individual soul (atman) and the universal soul (brahman) are linked, being the product of the same creation. The word *yoga* itself comes from the root *yug,* meaning bond, tie or yoke; and the principle underlying the exercises which it contains is intended precisely to link the human being to the cosmic energies. Our word *religion* derives from the Latin *religare,* and thus has a similar basic meaning—without, however, the techniques for producing self-awareness.

2. The myth of creation

What, then, has love got to do with all this? It is, precisely, present everywhere. Without Desire, the primordial Being Prajapati (the Purusha, or "he of every beginning") would not have wanted to father creation. Here we shall quote one of the amusing myths on the subject which exist in several versions.

"The Sole Being was unhappy with his solitary state and began to look for a second being. Then he became as big as a man and a woman locked in an embrace. He divided that body, which was himself, into two parts, which became husband and wife..."

"That is why the human body—at least before man takes a woman—is like the two halves of a split pea... He was united with her and mankind was born of their union.

"Then she thought: "How can he, having engendered me from himself, then be united with me? Clearly I must hide"! Whereupon she turned into a cow; but he became a bull, mated with her and brought cattle into being. She then turned into a mare, and he became a stallion ; she turned into a female donkey, and he became a mule: goats and sheep were thus created. In this way he produced everything which exists in pairs, down to the ants.

"He then acknowledged his powers: "In actual fact I am myself creation, as I have produced the entire world". In his way he came to be called Creation."

As in all comogonies, a Primordial Desire, a wish to create, lies at the basis of our universe, its forms and beings. Each part of the whole is linked to the others by a sort of chromosomic, cellular vital chain which is Life itself. That Life would not exist were it not for the desire to live, to procreate and to continue the chain of evolution. In other Indian myths we find the concept of a golden egg floating on the waters of non-being, fertilizing those waters and thus engendering existence. Which ever version one considers the movement of Genesis is always seen to involve a sort of sexual interplay between two complementary entities, a calorific rubbing, a penetration, a churning (as in one of the best-known myths, in which the primordial mountain Mandara "churns" the infinite ocean of milk), always the image of union, of a fertile osmosis which transforms the couple into a new energy. One plus two equals three, and so on endlessly from this beginning. It is interesting to note that none of these myths clash with the findings of modern science, according to which life emerged after a very slow process of chemical and electrical reactions within the mass of molecules of the primordial ocean.

3. The god and his shakti

Three principal gods eventually consolidated their power over all the other gods and beings and over Nature: they form the Trimurti, an entity truly constituting a form of energy. They are Brahma, the creator, Vishnu the protector and Shiva the destroyer; in this way the birth-life-death cycle which is present throughout all stages of our life, is rendered and governs the whole process. Each of these gods is accompanied by a shakti, which is both its female double and its power of manifestation. These "divine Mothers" are unanimously respected in India and each woman is regarded as their incarnation since she can herself be a mother and a procreator... the place, the means and the refuge of the continuity of creation. We can thus see the extent to which amorous relations, as described in the Kama Sutra, are imbued with respect and indissolubly bind spirit and matter together.

The whole of Indian culture and spirituality bear the imprint of eroticism; but it is a naturally codified eroticism, unlike the disembodied, suppressed variety to be found in our Western cultures. The lingas (stone phalluses) and their yonis (vulvas) of which there are tens of millions are universally respected throughout the Indian subcontinent, as a sign of respect for the organ of creation and the womb, the source of life.

Krishna, the favorite god of the pantheon (and the incarnation of Vishnu) was famous for his love for the Gopis, the legendary shepherdesses who worshipped him, and to whom he taught genuine communion with the divine essence, transcending and at the same time proceeding through physical love. He seduced the shepherdesses one by one, danced and played with them and loved them; then, just as each of them imagined she possessed him he would disappear, thus showing that life was governed by an illusion and that ideal love must go beyond the desire for possession. Everything is a *lila*, a game, while living forms are nothing more than a reflection of its divine form.

Hinduism proved able to ennoble sexual intercourse, both within and beyond the couple, on condition that the partners should see in themselves and their motions the effect of essentially divine fundamental energies; the act of love thus reproduces the first stages of the creation of the world, as the male principle becomes united to its complement, the shakti, or feminine principle.

Then comes the erotic union, which is both transphysiological and transpsychic, in which the man and the woman embody their divine status in the act, which can and should be made to last a long time and take whatever forms the lovers choose.

The woman gives her enjoyment to the man, while he gives her his strength, which is extended, though not emitted, within her body. The texts emphasize the fact that "he who has immobilized the essence of his spirit through identity of enjoyment in the state of the Innate One, instantly becomes a magician; he fears neither old age nor death. Anyone who secures a strong lock to the entrance of the breath and makes the spirit a lamp shining in the consequent terrible darkness, while enabling the jewel of the jina to touch the supreme heaven, as Kanha has said, reaches the nirvana while enjoying existence".

4. Preserving the seed

All oriental treatises on love advise against repeated ejaculation; the man is thus able to conserve his vigor while not wasting it needlessly, to acquire self-control with the much vaster potential for action and heightened psychosomatic energy which it produces and to come into contact with the reality of the present moment, the here and now. The satisfaction of his partner which radiates from his rock-like male sexual force opens up endless opportunities for him and also for her in the act of love. This is a union of constraints, blended in a timeless unity and leading to a higher stage of awareness contained in its own "void". In Indian tradition, this moment of absolute concentration which carnal love can and should provide, this moment of communion during which two beings find each other is the moment of highest respect: opposing and complementary forces mesh in the same act, beyond thought itself, in the same cosmic dance as at the beginning of creation. It is a participation in the movement of the world, a link to the vital urge, and a phase in awareness of oneself and of the universe.

About the time the Kama Sutra was written, new theories, having practical applications, began to develop from the ancient sacred Vedic traditions and their awareness techniques; these new roots were to lead to a genuine sexual yoga known as tantrism. This notion derives from the word *tantra* which means "expansion", in this case that of the faculties of the body and the awareness of the mind. One tantric text says that: "One should raise oneself by means of that which causes one to fall. The very aspects of our nature which impede us can be the cornerstones of our liberation." In such an approach the sexual impulses become a path opening up the realities of the cosmos and pointing to the unity of the finite and infinite.

As it developed, the ritual of the tantric asanas gave rise to an impressive series of psychophysical practices promoting the type of discipline which leads to meditation. In performing the asana the man and the woman are united, and its fulfilment lies in the experience of joy. During intercourse, those skilled in this art withdraw their awareness of the environment. The spirit aspires to be free. Retention heightens the pressure of sexual energy, raising it to incandescence, so that the psychic flow is released.

5. Tantrism

The Tantra asana shows the way to control over one's sexual energy for the promotion of sexual fulfilment. It teaches us to explore our senses rather than to tame them.

We shall refer also to the ten aspects (or steps) which tantric symbolism ascribes to the shakti, or feminine phase of cosmic energy. They are as follows:
1. Kali, the power of time.
2. Tara, the power of procreation.
3. Sodasi, the incarnation of the sixteen forms of desire.
4. Bhuvanesvari, the substantial forces of the material world.
5. Bhairavi, multiplied in an infinite number of forms and beings.
6. Chinnamasta, the distributor of vital energy in the cosmos.
7. Dhamabati, associated with frustrated desires.
8. Bagala, destroyer of negative forces.
9. Matangi, the power to dominate.
10. Kamala, the state of restored unity.

The tantras constantly emphasize that those who make love for erotic reasons alone are merely abusing themselves and run the risk of losing their vital energy. On the other hand, to the extent that one engages in sexual pleasures with an intense awareness of the spiritual (Goethe would call them "elective") affinities between the partners, if one disregards the call of the ego, then the act of love assumes its full liberating dimension. Only then can the existential awareness of unity become unveiled and realized in the notion proclaimed by all mystics:
"There is no difference between You and Me".

Maithuna, the yoga of love, makes it possible:
—to awaken the Kundalini, the symbolic serpent coiled at the base of the vertebral column which is the form of latent energy available to us and which is at work in our vertebral columns (our vital axis) and in our nerves in a highly uncontrolled way;
—to to learn how to use one's Prana, or breath of life, which is the same as that of the universe;
—to become blended with each other so as to die to oneself; and then to live again with a heightened awareness of the world around one.

6. The sexual act as an honor

In this way the sexual act is not relegated to the shadows of the unconscious and its phantoms; instead it is magnified, and illuminated with a light which properly displays all its countless facets. The Kama Sutra is therefore an illustrative educational manual which, though written for one particular type of society, carries a message of great relevance to our modern world: its refined sentiments, gentle preliminary voluptuousness and a variety of shared postures amount to a set of esthetic precepts conducive to pleasure. This is a romanticism of enjoyment which acquires its full meaning when interwoven with the superb miniatures offered in this book. This is a Kama Sutra such as has never been published before: it is a tribute to the magic of love, a practical guide, a virtuoso display of the art of seduction, and introduction to the fairyland of an ancient culture, a study in morality and a hymn to life; may this selection of texts and illustrations truly convey this centuries-old wisdom which held that eroticism should properly transcend the purely physical and merge with that cosmic energy which moves us just as it moves life and the orbits of the celestial bodies.

Marc de Smedt

"Her shapely back is as lithe as a serpent;
it blends harmoniously with her buttocks and her broad hips,
which resemble the bust of the green dove."

Four types of women and the qualities peculiar to each

Generally speaking Indian authors divide women into four categories, according to their physical and moral characteristics.

The perfect type is the Padmini, or Lotus Woman; there is virtually no kind of merit which is not attributed to her. Here is a summary of them:

She is as beautiful as a lotus bud, like Rathi (desire). Her slender waist contrasts nicely with the fullness of her hips. She has the carriage of a swan and walks gently and gracefully.

Her supple and elegant body has the scent of sandalwood; it is upright and svelte like the ciricha tree and has the sheen of the mirobolam stem.

Her tender, smooth skin is soft to the touch, like the trunk of a young elephant. It has the color of gold and sparkles like lightning.

Her voice is the song of the male kolika enchanting its mate; her words are of ambrosia.

Her sweat has the odor of musk; she naturally exhales more perfumes than any other woman. The bees follow her like a sweet honey-scented flower.

Her long, curled silken hair, which is itself aromatic, black like the bees, makes a delightful frame for her face, which resembles the disk of the full moon, and falls in jade strands over her rich shoulders.

Her forehead is pure; her well-arched eyebrows are two crescents; when slightly moved by emotion they far transcend the arc of Kama.

Her finely shaped eyes are shining, gentle and timid like those of the gazelle, and red in the corners. The eyeballs, black as night deep inside their orbits, sparkle like stars in a dark sky. Her long silken lashes lend a fascinating softness to her gaze.

Her nose, which resembles the sesame bud, is straight and then becomes rounded like a parrot's beak.

Her voluptuous lips are pink like a flower bud which is about to open or red like coral or the fruit of the bimba.

Her teeth, which are white as the jasmine of Arabia, have the sheen of ivory; when she smiles, they appear like a string of pearls mounted on coral.

Her round polished neck is like a golden tower. Her shoulders are attached to it by fine bonds, as well as to her superbly molded arms which are like the stem of the mango tree, ending in two delicate hands which remind one of the branches of the ashoka tree.

Her full and firm breasts are like the fruit of the vilva; they are like two upturned cups of gold crowned with the bud of the pomegranate flower.

Her shapely back is as lithe as a serpent; it blends harmoniously with her buttocks and her broad hips, which resemble the bust of the green dove.

Her deep navel, shining like a ripe berry, can be seen on her pure, delicately rounded jagdana (belly). The skin around her waist forms a belt made of three graceful folds just above the hips.

Her buttocks are marvelous; she is a Nitambini (the nymph Sakuntala was a Nitambini).

Like the lotus blooming in the shade of a tender patch of kusha grass (the sacred grass *par excellence*), her small yoni opens mysteriously under the pubis sheltered by a hairy veil six inches across.

*"She enjoys the pleasures of love with her husband and knows how to excite his desire by means of caresses.
The god of love would be in ecstasy at her side."*

Her loveseed is perfumed like a freshly blooming lily; her firm, plump round thighs are like the stem of a young banana tree.

Her tiny, dainty feet are finely joined to her legs, like two lotus flowers.

When she bathes in a sacred pool her every gesture speaks of love; the gods would be troubled to see her at play in the water.

Pearls tremble on her ears; on her bosom there rests a necklace of precious stones. Her beauty is enhanced by ornaments—few in number—on her arms and ankles.

She likes white garments, white flowers, fine jewels and rich apparel. She wears a garment made of three layers of striped muslin.

As delicate as the betel flower, she is fond of sweet, pure and light food; she eats but little and sleeps lightly.

She is well versed in the thirty-two musical modes of Radha; like the lover of Krishna she sings harmoniously accompanying herself on the vina, which she plays with graceful strokes of her slender, agile fingers.

When she dances, the supple and harmonious motion of her arms form the most graceful curves, almost, at times, as if she wanted to hide her personal charms, for her modesty is very great (in India women always dance alone).

Her conversation is pleasant and her smile spreads bliss around her; she is mischievous, playful and fond of pleasure.

She excels in the tasks which are hers.

She avoids the society of dishonest people and does her duty scrupulously; lying is alien to her.

She constantly adores and worships the Brahmans, her father and the gods; she seeks out the conversation of the Brahmans; she is liberal towards them and charitable towards the poor, for whose sake she would willingly relinquish her husband's wealth.

She enjoys the pleasures of love with her husband and knows how to excite his desire by means of caresses.

The god of love would be in ecstasy at her side.

She is highly affectionate towards her husband and will show such tenderness to no other man. All her speech is imbued with fondness, and she is absolutely devoted to her husband. She is perfect in all respects.

One should add to this already flattering portrait some of the many phrases used by the poets in honor of the Padmini:

Treasure of love! Unbounded tenderness! Woman who loves but feels no desire! Woman whose happiness is manifest! Woman like Rathi (desire), wife of Ananya (love), who bows under the weight of her well rounded bosom! Woman whose love intoxicates!

After the Padmini comes the Chitrini, or Art Woman.

The Chitrini has a quick mind, and a light, vivacious temperament. She resembles the Lotus, her throat is firm; her hair, woven in a single plait, falls over her rich shoulders like black serpents; her voice has the sweetness of ambrosia; her hips are narrow, while her gentle smooth thighs have the roundness of a banana tree stem; her gait is that of a playful elephant; she loves pleasure, and is capable of both arousing and varying it.

The Hastini (name of the elephant) occupies the third place.

The Hastini has abundant hair which shines and hangs in long silken curls; her gaze would embarrass the god

of love and bring a blush to the cheeks of the shepherd girls. The body of this graceful woman is like a golden liana, her earrings are studded with stones and her garments are decorated with flowers. Her firm, well rounded breasts resemble a pair of golden vases.

The last type is the Sankhini (sow).

Her hair is plaited and coiled about her head; her face, which carries an expression of passion, is misshapen; her body is like that of a pig. She always seems to be angry, scolding and complaining.

Her breasts and her belly smell of fish.

She is unclean; she eats anything at all, and sleeps to excess. Her eyes are always dull and bleary.

Four types of man correspond, as lovers or husbands, to these four types of woman.

The Hare Man, who is active, lively and alert, is for the Padmini.

The Stag Man, who seeks affection in sexual intercourse, is for the Chitrini.

The Bull Man, having the strength and the temperament of the animal in question, is for the Hastini.

The Horse Man, who has the vigor and the sprightliness of a stallion, is for the Sankhini.

According to the poets, there is one Padmini for every ten million women, one Chitrini for every ten thousand, one Hastini for every thousand, while the Sankhini is to be found everywhere.

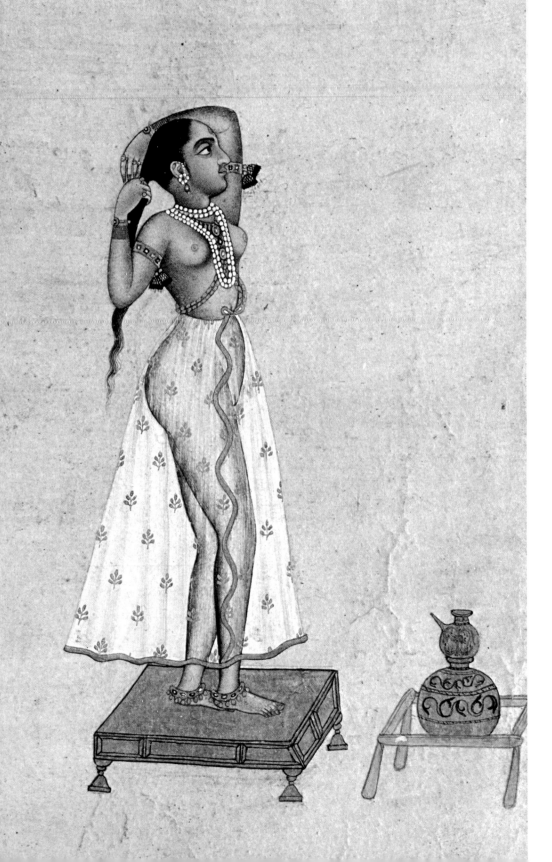

Conversation

It often happened that conversations took the form of exchanges of poetic improvisations and quotations between competing poets.

The following dialogue has been devised to give the reader a sample of this sort of conversation:

A wise Brahman: "Who made this maze of uncertainty, this temple of immodesty, this receptacle of defects, this field sown with a thousand deceits, this barrier to the gates of heaven, this mouth of the infernal city, this poison which has the scent of ambrosia, this cord which ties mortals to the earthly world—in a word, woman?"

A courtesan: "The false sage who curses women is deceiving himself and others; for the fruit of penitence is heaven and heaven offers the Apsaras to those who achieve it."

The Brahman: "Women have honey in their words and poison in their hearts; that is why one sucks their lips while one strikes their chest with the back of one's hand."

The courtesan: "The madmen who flee from women obtain only bitter fruit; their stupidity and the god of love punish them cruelly. The day when honorable men succeed in mastering their senses, the Vindhyas mountains will swim across the oceans."

The Brahman: "On this earth there is only a garden full of pernicious flowers, which is youth; it is the seat of passion, the cause of suffering more intense than that of a hundred hells, the germ of madness, the curtain of cloud which covers the light of learning, the sole weapon of the god of love, the chain of defects of all sorts."

The courtesan: "An old one-eyed dog, limping and mangy, with only skin and bone, his mouth torn by the potsherds which he gnaws, still runs after bitches; the god of love continues to torment men, even as death approaches. When the ashoka tree is touched by the foot of a beautiful woman its flowers bloom at once.

Voluptuous women inflame the hearts of all men with their lascivious graces; they chat with one man, dart provocative glances at another and a third occupies their heart."

The Brahman: "He who, with control over his senses, has merged his awareness with the supreme soul cares nothing for the prattling of mistresses, the honey of their lips, the moon of their face and the love games, replete with sighs, in which their plump bosoms take part."

The courtesan: "The only men who talk of renouncing love are the scholars who constantly have the sacred scriptures at the tip of the tongue, yet even they do not mean what they say.

Who could flee from the hips of beautiful young women adorned with resonant belts strung with red beads?

Even Brahma does not have the courage to withstand the acts of a woman in the state of passion."

A mature man: "Man can be sure of his honor, virtue and wisdom only when his heart and his firmness of resolve have successfully withstood the onslaught of female corruption.

How many men who could not have been bought by all the gold in the world have succumbed to their temptations!"

A young man: "What is the most beautiful of sights?

The face of a young woman in love.

What is the softest of perfumes? Her sweet breath.

"A faint smile on their lips, their glances at once timid and bold, their joyous chatter, flight and sudden return, continual frolicking — young women with the eyes of the gazelle are a constant delight in everything they do."

What is the most agreeable of sounds? The voice of the loved one.

What is the most exquisite of tastes? The dew which moistens her lips.

What is softest to the touch? Her body.

What is the most pleasant picture a man can conjure up in his kind? That of her charms.

Everything about a young woman in love is appealing."

A young poet: "The young virgin is like the tender bud of a rose which has yet to bloom; in all its purity it grows in peace in the shadow of the protective thicket, safe from danger; yet once her unveiled bosom has lent itself to the kisses of the seductive nightingale it is soon thereafter separated from the maternal stem and ignobly associated with the grass over which the common masses might walk, it is exposed to the passers-by in public places; when it has thus been dulled by a thousand impure kisses, one seeks in vain its original freshness."

Another young man: "A faint smile on their lips, their glances, at once timid and bold, their joyous chatter, flight and sudden return, continual frolicking—young women with the eyes of the gazelle are a constant delight in everything they do.

When they are away we long to see them return.

When we see them we have only one desire, to feel their embrace.

When we are in their arms, we can no longer tear ourselves away from them."

The young poet: "What mortal is destined to receive such ravishing beauty, as fresh as a flower whose scent has never been inhaled and whose fine down has never been touched, a tender bud which no mortal has dared break off from its stem, or a pearl still pure inside the protective mother-of-pearl where it was born?"

20

The elegant life: lovers' meetings

The dwelling must be well situated, along the banks of some clean watercourse, in a city or town, or some place where people go for recreation.

The inner rooms must be placed towards the back of the building, the reception rooms in front, and all must be comfortably furnished and tastefully decorated.

Hygiene. Every day one must take a bath and rub one's body with oil. Every three days lac should be applied to the whole body; every four days the head must be shaved, and, once every five or ten days, the whole body.

Timetable. Three meals a day, in the morning, at noon and at night; a bath and a midday sleep; elegant white clothes; flowers, an aviary; in the morning, some games and pastimes with parasites, and an afternoon passed with friends.

After breakfast a speech lesson to parrots and other birds, followed by fights between cocks, quails or pigeons.

In the evening, singing: then the master of the house, with his friends, in a suitably ornate and scented reception room, awaits the arrival of his mistress; when she arrives she is received with the customary courtesies, and engages in a loving and agreeable conversation with all present.

When she is to spend the night in the house of her lover, she comes already bathed, perfumed and suitably dressed. Her lover offers her refreshments; he invites her to sit on his left, takes her hair in his hands, touches the hem and the knot of her lower garment and puts his right arm gently around her waist. A relaxed and pleasant conversation then ensues, with many gay and witty remarks, and erotic or amorous stories are told. The assembled company then sings, with or without gestures; and there is music and much excited drinking.

Eventually, when the woman, aroused by such erotic stimulation, betrays her own desires, the master of the household invites his guests to leave, giving them flowers, bouquets and betel leaves.

The two lovers then remain alone. Having had their fill of pleasure, they modestly rise and, without so much as a glance at each other, go separately to the toilet which is, in India, the bathroom.

They then come back to sit together and chew betel leaves. Then the man, with his own hand, rubs the body of the woman with an ointment of pure sandalwood or some other aromatic essence; next he puts his left arm around her while saying sweet things to her, and he gives her a stimulating scented drink from a cup which he holds in his left hand. Together they eat cakes and sweetmeats, sip broths and gruel soup and drink fresh coconut milk, sherbets, mango juice and sweetened lemon juice; lastly, undisturbed by intruders, they savor the finest, sweetest and purest produce of the country.

The two lovers often go up to the terrace of the house where they enjoy the moonlight as they chat pleasantly together. Then, as the woman reclines on his knees, her face towards the moon, the lover points out to her the various planets, the morning star, the polar star and the constellations.

Different types of sexual intercourse

There are seven types of intercourse:

'*Spontaneous intercourse.*' Two persons love each other and unite their bodies out of sympathy and mutual attraction.

Barthiari says that love play, in the case of a woman of good birth, is full of charm. First the woman says "no! no!", and feigns disdain for her lover's caresses; then her desire is aroused, though some shreds of modesty remain; then her resistance slackens and her firmness is discarded; lastly she feels keenly the secret pleasure of amorous ardor; setting aside all restraint she savors an ineffable bliss which causes her limbs to become tense.

'*Intercourse of ardent love*'. The man and the woman have loved each other for some time and have found it difficult to meet; or one of the lovers comes back from a journey, or two lovers are reconciled after a quarrel.

In this case the two lovers are burning with an impatient desire to be united and give each other complete satisfaction.

'*Intercourse for nascent love*'. This takes place between two partners whose love is still only a seed.

'*Intercourse of artificial love*'. Here the man performs the sexual act only by exciting himself through the accessory means referred to in the Kama Sutra—kisses, embraces—or the man and woman unite their bodies without love, the heart of each of them being elsewhere. In this case they must make use of all the methods for generating excitement taught by the Kama Shastra.

'*Intercourse of love*'. One of the two partners, throughout the entire act, imagines that he is in the arms of another person whom he truly loves.

'*Intercourse of eunuchs*'. The woman is a water-bearer or a servant of a caste lower than that of the man, so the sexual act lasts only long enough to extinguish the man's desire. In this case there are no preliminary or accessory acts.

'*Deceitful intercourse*'. Between a courtesan and a peasant, or between a well-educated man and a peasant woman; it is limited to a brutal act, unless the woman is very beautiful.

24

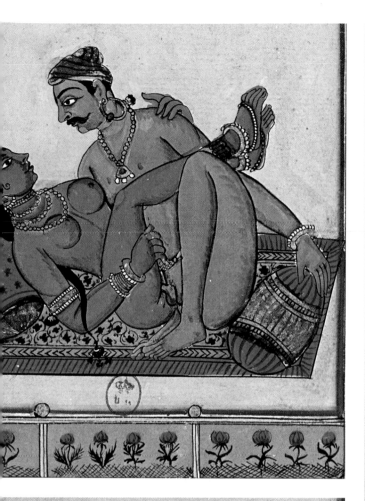

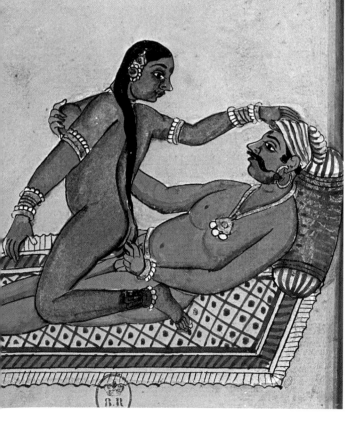

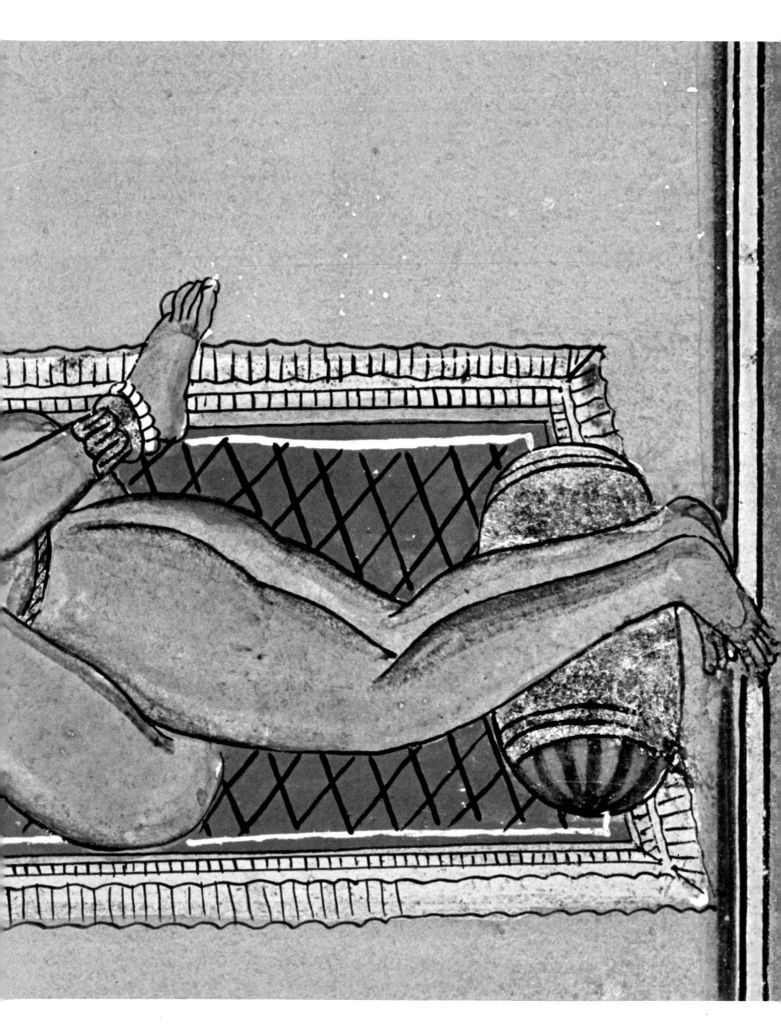

Caresses which precede or accompany the sexual act

During their early meetings it is recommended that lovers avoid a great deal of kissing, embracing and other accessories of the sexual act; though one can be lavish with such things on subsequent occasions.

One can kiss the forehead, the eyes, the cheeks, the throat, the chest, the breasts, the lips and the inside of the mouth.

The inhabitants of the East also kiss their women at the joints of the thighs, on the arms and on the navel.

With a young woman there are three sorts of kiss;

The 'nominal', the 'moving' and the 'touching'.

The 'nominal' is a plain kiss on the mouth, as the lips of the two lovers are brought into contact.

In the 'moving kiss' the girl squeezes her lover's lower lip between her lips; she draws it into her mouth with a sort of sucking motion.

In the 'touching kiss' she touches her lover's lip with her tongue, while closing her eyes, and places her two hands in his.

Authors also refer to four other types of kiss:

'Straight', 'bent', 'turned' and 'pressed'.

In the 'straight kiss' the two lips are applied directly, those of the lover on those of his mistress.

In the 'bent kiss' the two lovers, their heads inclined, bend their lips towards each other.

In the 'turned kiss' one of the lovers turns the other's head towards him with his hand, while holding his partner's chin with the other hand.

A kiss is said to be 'pressed' when one of the partners presses the lower lip of the other person with his two lips. It is said to be 'very pressed', when, having taken the lips between two fingers the lover touches it with his tongue and presses it hard with one lip.

Lovers vie with each other to see who shall be first to seize the lower lip of the other partner between his own lips. If the woman loses she must cry out, repel her lover and beat the air with her hands, challenging him to another bout. If she loses a second time her resentment must be seen to be even greater: she must take advantage of a moment's inattention on the part of the man, or wait until he is asleep, to seize his lower lip between her teeth, gripping it so hard that he cannot work himself free. Once that is done she starts laughing, shouting and mocking her lover; she dances and jumps about in front of him, jesting and saying whatever occurs to her: she frowns and makes eyes at him.

These are the games and wagers in which lovers engage when kissing.

Very passionate lovers do the same with the other affectations which we shall consider later on.

When the man kisses the upper lip of the woman while she, in return, kisses his lower lip, it is the 'kiss of the upper lip'.

When one of the lovers takes in his lips the lips of his partner, it is the 'clasping kiss'.

When, during this kiss, his tongue touches the teeth and palate of the other person, it is called the 'fight of the tongue'.

The kiss should be moderate, contracted, pressed or soft, depending on the part of the body to which it is

applied.

The range of kisses can also be said to include sucking on the nipples—an act which, in the songs of the Bayaderes of southern India, is mentioned as a natural prelude to intercourse.

When a woman kisses the face of her sleeping lover, it is the 'kiss that kindles love'.

When a woman kisses her lover while he is distracted or busy, it is the 'kiss that turns away'.

When a lover comes home late and finds his mistress in bed and kisses her as she sleeps, thus expressing his desire for her, it is the 'kiss that awakens'. In such a case, the woman may feign sleep when her lover arrives, in order to elicit this kiss.

When one kisses the image of a person reflected in a mirror or in water, or his own shadow on a wall, it is the 'kiss of declaration'.

When one kisses a child sitting on one's knees, or a picture of a statue, in the presence of the loved person, it is the 'transferred kiss'.

When at night, at a theater or in a gathering of men of caste, a man approaches a woman and kisses one of her fingers (if she is standing) or her toes (if she is seated), or when a woman, while massaging her lover's body, lays her face on his thigh, as if wishing to make it a pillow so as to arouse his desires, and kisses his thigh or big toe, it is the 'provocative kiss'.

The following verses have been quoted about these kisses:

"Whatever one of the lovers may do to the other, the same should be returned by that other person; kiss for kiss, caress for caress, blow for blow."

*"The rules of the Shastra should be observed
as long as the passion is moderate;
but once the wheel of love begins to turn,
neither Shastra nor order should be followed."*

The embrace

The embrace, whereby lovers show their fondness for each other, is of four kinds: 'touching', 'piercing', 'rubbing' and 'pressing'.

The first of these takes place when a man, on some pretext or other, places himself next to or in front of a woman so that their bodies come into contact.

The 'piercing embrace' occurs when, in some solitary place, a woman bends down to pick something up, and as it were pierces a man with her breasts; the man, for his part, takes hold of her and squeezes her.

These first two kinds of embrace are performed between persons who are unable to see or freely contact each other.

The third embrace takes place when two persons who are walking slowly in the dark or in some isolated place rub their bodies together.

When, in similar circumstances, one of the lovers presses the other's body hard against a wall or a pillar, it is the 'pressing embrace'.

These last two contacts are carried out by common agreement.

When lovers meet they may make partial embraces: face against face, breast against breast, jagdana against jagdana (area between the navel and the thighs), thighs against thighs, and also embraces of the whole body, with all sorts of fond gestures, the woman letting her hair flow loosely.

These embraces have the following names: 'creeper', 'climbing a tree', 'mixture of sesame seed and rice' and the 'water and milk embrace'.

In the first two of these the man is standing, while the latter two are an actual part of intercourse.

In the first, the woman clings to the man as the ivy clings to the tree; she inclines her head on his to kiss, while uttering faint cries of "sut! sut!"; she embraces him and looks at him lovingly.

In the second, the woman places one foot on the man's foot and the other on his thigh, putting one of her arms around his back and the other on his shoulders, and sings and coos softly, apparently wishing to climb up to receive a kiss.

In the third, the man and the woman are lying down, embracing each other so tightly that their thighs and arms are interwoven like two creepers, and are rubbing against each other.

In the fourth, the man and the woman are in such ecstasy that they are rendered oblivious to everything; they neither fear nor feel pain or injury; penetrating each other fully, they now form only a single body, one flesh, whether the man has the woman sitting on his knees, or on her side, or facing him, on a bed.

A poet has written the following aphorism about this:

"It is good to learn and to discuss the embraces, since this is a way of arousing desire; but in the sexual act itself one should engage even in those which are not mentioned in the Kama Shastra, as long as they heighten one's love and passion."

The rules of the Shastra should be observed as long as the passion is moderate; but once the wheel of love begins to turn, neither Shastra nor order should be followed.

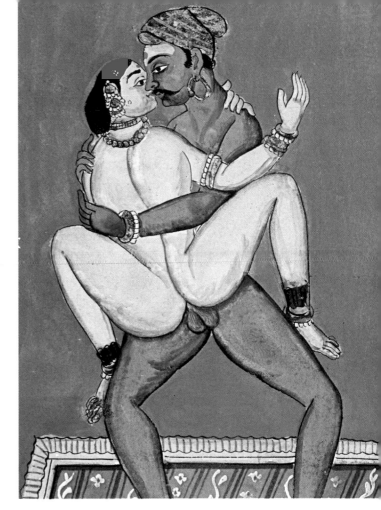
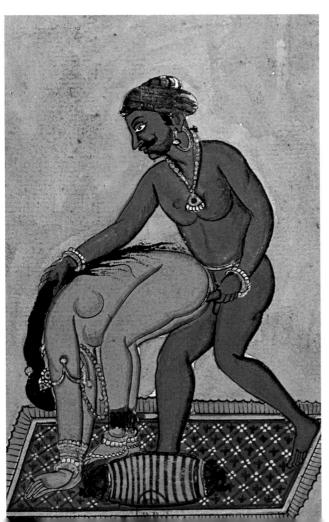
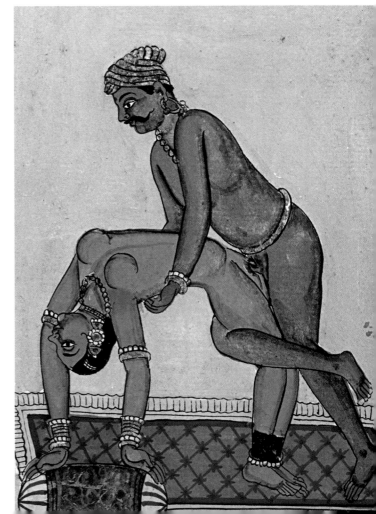

Pressing, rubbing, scratching and marks made with the nails.

Generally speaking marks made with the nails should be imprinted on the armpits, the throat, the breasts, the lips, the jagdana or midriff, and the thighs.

These, quite as much as bites, are singular—and sometimes feigned—evidence of love between intensely passionate lovers. They exchange these gestures at their first meeting, when leaving on a journey, on their return, during a reconciliation, and, lastly, when the woman is, for whatever reason, intoxicated.

The nails can be used to make eight marks, by scratching or pressing: 'sounding', 'half-moon', the 'circle', the 'lines', the 'tiger's nail or claw mark', the 'peacock's foot', the 'hare's leap' and the 'blue lotus leaf'.

'Sounding' is done by pressing the chin, the breasts, the lower lip or the jagdana so softly as not to make any mark or scratch, and only in order that the hair will stand up through contact with the nails, the scratching of which can be heard.

A lover can do this with a young woman when he is massaging her or gently scratching her head, and when he wants to frighten her or disturb her

The 'half-moon' is the curve of a single nail imprinted on the neck or breasts.

The 'circle' is a set of two facing half-moons. This mark is usually made on the navel, in the small dimples which form around the buttocks in the standing posture, and in the groin.

The 'line' is a short line made by the nail on any part of the body.

The 'tiger's claw' is a curved line made on the breast.

The 'peacock's foot' is a similar curve made on the breast with the five nails: this type of scratching requires real mastery.

In the 'hare's leap' the mark of the five nails is made near one of the nipples.

The 'blue lotus leaf' consists of marks made on the breasts or the hips in the form of lotus leaves.

There are also other marks; indeed there is no end to them, for, as an ancient author says: "The art of imprinting the marks of love is familiar to all".

Vatsyayana adds: "Just as variety is necessary in love, so also variety, in its turn, generates love".

That is why the courtesans, who are fully versed in everything pertaining to love, are so desirable.

Nail marks may not be made on married women; however it is permitted to make special marks on the hidden parts of their bodies, as a fond memory and in order to heighten one's love.

Even when they are old and have almost been effaced, nail marks remind a woman of previous moments of love and revive her passion, which might otherwise be simply lost.

A young woman on whose breasts such marks are to be seen can impress even a stranger who sees her from a distance.

A man who bears nail and teeth marks on his body is successful with women, even those who resist love.

34

*"When a lover bites his mistress hard,
she must, with feigned anger,
bite him back twice as hard."*

Bites

One may bite all those parts of the body which are kissed, except for the lower lip, the inside of the mouth and the eyes.

The qualities sought after in teeth are: brilliance, evenness, the right proportions, sharp tips.

Defective teeth are rough, soft, big and loose.

There are various kinds of bites:

The 'hidden bite' leaves on the skin only a passing redness.

The 'swollen bite' occurs when the skin has been seized and pulled, as though with pincers.

The 'point' is when a very small area of skin has been seized by only two teeth.

'Coral and jewel': the skin is squeezed simultaneously by the teeth (the jewels) and the lips (the coral).

The 'line of jewels' is formed by a bite involving all the teeth.

The 'broken cloud' is a broken line of points undulating around a curve, due to the space between the teeth.

The 'bite of the boar' is imprinted on the breasts and the shoulders and consists of two lines of teeth marks, one above the other, with a red gap.

The first three bites are made on the lower lip: the line of points and the jewels are imprinted on the throat, the dimple of the neck and the groin.

The plain line of points is imprinted on the forehead and the thighs.

The 'swollen bite' and the 'coral and jewel bite' are always made on the left cheek, on which nail and teeth marks are considered to be fine ornaments.

One can convey one's desire to a woman by making nail or teeth marks on the following objects which she wears or owns: any ornament of the forehead or ears, a bunch of flowers, and a betel or tamala leaf.

Here are some verses about this:

"When a lover bites his mistress hard, she must, with feigned anger, bite him back twice as hard".

This means that, for a point, she will return a line of points, and for a line of points a broken cloud.

If she is very excited, and because of his passionate condition starts a kind of fight with her lover, she will take him by the hair, pull his head towards her and bite his lower lip; then, in her delirium, she will bite him all over his body, with her eyes closed.

And even in daytime and in public, when her lover shows her some mark that she has made on him, she must smile at the sight of it, turn her head towards him as if to scold him, and then, feigning irritation, show him the marks he has made on her.

When two lovers behave in this way, their passion will last for ages without slackening.

The various ways of striking and the corresponding sounds

Blows are a form of love play.

Sexual intercourse can be compared to a dispute, because of the thousand contrarieties of love and the ease with which lovers quarrel.

The parts of the body which may be struck out of passion are: the shoulders, the head, the chest between the breasts, the back, the jagdana, the hips and the sides.

Such blows may be administered with the back of the hand, with the fingers together like a pad, with the palm of the hand and with the fist.

When the woman is struck she makes various hissing noises and any of eight sounds: 'phra', 'phat', 'sut' and 'plat'; the thundering, cooing and weeping sounds, and the sound 'hin'.

The sound 'phat' is like the splitting of bamboo.

The sound 'phut' is like something falling into the water.

The woman also says certain words, such as 'mother', 'father', etc.

Sometimes the sounds or words used express defense, the desire for separation, pain or approval.

To these assorted exclamations one may add the imitation of the buzzing of bees, the cooing of the dove, and cuckoo, the call of the parrot or the sparrow, the hissing of the duck, and the sounds of the quail and the peacock.

Punches may be applied to the back of the woman while she is seated on the man's knees; she must respond by feigning anger and uttering the cooing and weeping sounds.

During intercourse it is customary to tap between the two breasts with the back of the hand, faster and faster as the level of excitement rises, until the end of the sexual act; at that point one should repeat the sound 'hin', or some other preferred sound.

When the man strikes the woman's head with the end of his fingers held tightly together, he utters the sound 'phat', while the woman replies with the cooing sound and 'phat' and 'phut'.

When kissing and other forms of love play begin, the woman should always hiss.

As the excitment grows, when the woman is not accustomed to such blows, she should continually utter the words "enough, enough!" ! "finish now!", as well as "mother", and "father", together with cries and moans, and the thundering and weeping sounds.

Towards the end of intercourse the man should press the palm of his hand hard against the woman's breasts, jagdana or sides, whereupon she should reply with the hissing of the goose, or the sound of the quail.

38

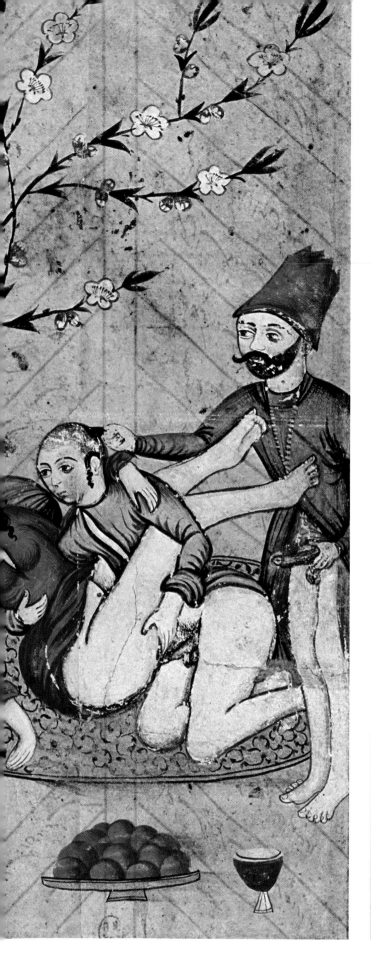

"The women of the Audhra region have delicate limbs and are highly salacious.
The women of Ganda are gentle in both language and body."

The sexual preferences of women in the various parts of India

The author gives information about the women from the different parts of India which is intended for men who might find themselves in need of it.

The women of the center, between the Ganges and the Jumma, have elevated feelings, and will under no circumstances allow any man to make nail or teeth marks on them.

The women of Avantika enjoy base pleasures and coarse behavior.

The women of Maharashtra love the sixty-four sorts of desire. They enjoy obscene remarks and are extremely passionate.

The women of Pataliputra (the modern Pathna) have the same capacity for passion as the latter, but do not display it in public.

Dravidian women, despite caresses of all sorts, take a long time to become passionate and are very slow to achieve their orgasm.

The women of Vanavasi are quite cold and unresponsive to caresses and bodily contact and will not tolerate obscene comments.

The women of Avanti are fond of all sorts of sexual intercourse, with the exception of the accessory caresses.

The women of Malva are fond of being kissed, embraced and, in particular, of being struck; they do not, however, like bites and scratches.

The women of the Punjab are deliriously fond of *auparishtaka* (caresses with the tongue, and lesbian pleasures).

The women of Aparatika and Lat are very passionate and are fond of uttering softly the sound 'sit'.

The women of Ouda are headstrong in their desires, their seed flows abundantly—indeed they stimulate its flow by taking medication.

The women of the Audhra region have delicate limbs and are highly salacious.

The women of Ganda are gentle in both body and language.

40

Man can be a hare, a bull or a stallion.
Woman can be a gazelle, a mare or an elephant.

Classification of men and women based on the size of their sexual organs

Men are divided into three classes, according to the dimensions of their linga.

Class No. 1 : Hare; No. 2: Bull; No. 3 : Stallion.

Women can also be divided into three classes corresponding to the dimensions of their yoni.

No. 1: Gazelle; No. 2: Mare; No. 3: Elephant.

In this way there are three equal forms of mating, between classes which correspond to each other, and six unequal, between classes which do not.

Mating between No. 2 (Bull) and No. 1 (Gazelle), or between No. 3 (Stallion) and No. 2 (Mare) is said to be superior.

That of No. 3 (Stallion) and No. 1 (Gazelle) is said to be very superior.

Mating of No. 1 (Hare) with No. 2 (Mare), or No. 2 (Bull) and No. 3 (Elephant) is said to be inferior.

The higher forms of mating are those which provide the greatest degree of pleasure.

Similarly, men and women can be classified according to the intensity of their orgasms: weak, medium and strong.

This criterion produces as many mating combinations as the preceding one.

There is, moreover, a third classification of a similar sort, which is based on the length of time it takes the man and woman to achieve orgasm; the same number of combinations is thus arrived at.

If the different numbers in these classification are combined, the total number of possibilities is very great.

It is the duty of men, and particularly of husbands, to use the means which are most suitable, in each case, for the successful completion of intercourse.

When a couple first performs the sexual act, the passion of the man is intense and reaches its culmination in a short time; the opposite tends to happen on subsequent occasions. The converse applies to women.

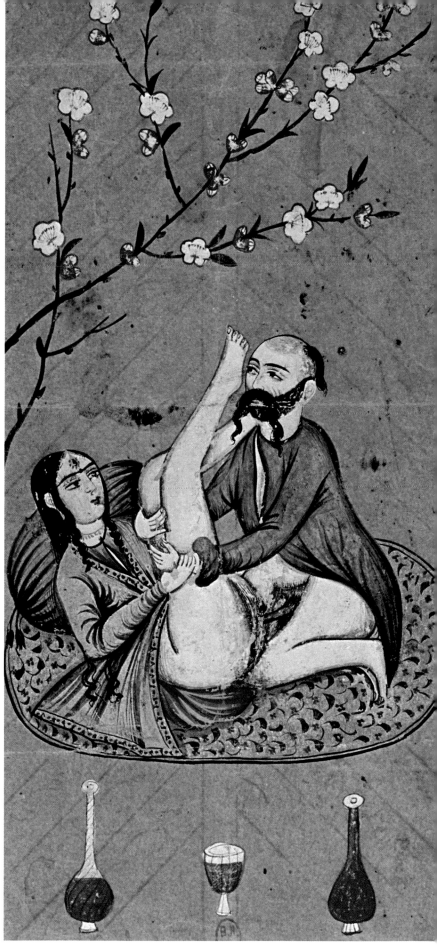

Various positions and postures conducive to conception, for use in the sexual act.

In superior intercourse the woman should place herself so that the yoni will be opened.

In equal intercourse she lies on her back in the natural position and lets the man make her a necklace with his arms.

In inferior intercourse she arranges herself so as to contract the yoni; she should also take medication to induce the orgasm earlier than would otherwise be the case.

For the Gazelle Woman, lying down, there are three positions:

'Wide open'. Her head is held very low, so as to raise the middle of the body. The man then has to apply saliva or some lubricant to either linga or yoni to facilitate penetration.

'Yawning'. The woman raises and parts her thighs.

'Position of the wife of Indra'. She crosses her feet over her thighs—an act which requires practice. This position is very suitable for very superior intercourse (Stallion with Gazelle).

For inferior and very inferior degrees of intercourse there are:

'Clasping position': the male partner, lying down, has his legs stretched out and applied directly to those of the female.

The position may be horizontal or on the side; in this latter position the man should lie on his left side.

This rule should be followed whenever the partners are lying down, regardless of the classification to which the woman belongs.

'Pressing position'. After intercourse has taken place in the clasping position, the woman squeezes her lover with her thighs.

'Twining position'. The woman places one of her thighs across the thigh of her lover.

'Position of the mare'. The woman holds the linga in her yoni, as in a vice. This is learnt only from practice and is done mainly among the women of the Andra region.

Souvarnanabha also mentions:

'Rising position'. The woman lifts her legs straight up.

'Yawning position'. The woman places both her legs on the man's shoulders.

44

'*Pressed position*'. The man presses to his body the two crossed and raised feet of the woman; if only one foot is raised, the position is known as 'half pressed'. The woman places one foot on the man's shoulder and stretches the other leg out to the side; then she assumes a similar pose on the opposite side, and so on, alternating.

'*Driving in the nail*'. One of the woman's legs is on the man's head and the other is stretched out to the side.

'*Position of the crab*'. Both the legs of the woman are drawn up and placed on her stomach.

'*Package*'. The woman lifts and crosses her thighs.

'*Lotus position*'. In this position the woman crosses her legs, keeping her thighs apart. This is the same as the 'position of the wife of Indra', referred to above.

'*Turning position*'. During intercourse, the man turns around the woman without becoming disengaged from her or interrupting the act, while the woman keeps his body embraced; this can be mastered only through practice.

It is easy and recommended, says Souvernanabha, to perform the sexual act in all the possible ways while in the bath; but Vatsyayana condemns any intercourse in water as being contrary to religious law.

When the woman gets down on her hands and feet like a quadruped, and her lover mounts her like a bull, it is called the 'mating of the cow'. In this position all the love play normally performed on the front of the body may be applied to the back. The man may also seize with his right hand the woman's breasts, while titillating the clitoris with his left and moving his linga inside the vagina; this augments the woman's desire and can accelerate the process of achieving orgasm, so that hers will coincide with that of the man.

This is the position in which the womb is best placed for conception, as its interior is lower than its orifice. It is also the most natural and least voluptuous position, as in it the clitoris is not touched, unless the man deliberately puts his hand on it.

*"An ingenious man
will use many different types of intercourse,
in imitation of the beasts and the birds."*

Attitudes designed exclusively to arouse desire

When the man and the woman perform the sexual act standing up, leaning against each other or against a wall or pillar, it is 'supported mating'.

When the man, with his back to the wall, raises and supports the woman who is seated on his joined hands and between his arms, while she, with her hands twined about his neck, embraces him with her thighs towards the middle of his body, and moves herself by her feet which are touching the wall against which the man is leaning, it is 'suspended mating'.

It is also possible to imitate the act of the dog, the goat, the deer, the forcible mounting and penetration of the donkey and the cat, the leap of the tiger, the rubbing of the boar, and the mounting of the mare by the stallion, by behaving exactly as those animals do with their females.

When a man caresses two women at the same time, it is known as 'double mating'. It can be done when two women lie on the edge of the bed, on top of each other, face to face like two lovers, with their legs dangling over the edge of the bed; the linga passes from one yoni to the other, in a succession of strokes, first *a recto,* and then *a retro.*

Simultaneous intercourse with several women is called 'mating with a herd of cows'.

There is also 'mating in the water', which is how elephants inseminate several females, apparently only in the water; 'mating with several goats', or 'mating with several gazelles', in other words, between the man and a number of females.

In the Gramanere, several young men enjoy a woman who may be the wife of one of them, either in turn or all at the same time. The woman is stretched out on top of one of them, another inserts his linga in her yoni, a third uses her mouth and a fourth embraces her middle part; and they go on in this way enjoying the various parts of her body alternately.

The same thing can be done when several men are in the company of a courtesan, or when there is only one courtesan to satisfy the needs of many men.

The reverse may be done by the women of the royal harem when they accidentally get hold of a man.

In southern India they practise 'low mating', which involves inserting the linga in the anus.

The following aphorism concludes this subject:

"An ingenious man will use many different types of intercourse, in imitation of the beasts and the birds, since these different methods, practised in accordance with the customs of each country and the tastes of individuals, evoke love, friendship and respect in women."

The role of the man in intercourse

The man must do his utmost to provide the woman with pleasure.

When the woman is on her bed and absorbed in his conversation, the man should undo the knot of her lower garment; if she resists, he will shut her mouth with kisses.

Many authors are of the opinion that he should begin by sucking the woman's nipples.

When his linga is erect he should touch her with his hands at various points and pleasantly caress the different parts of her body.

If the woman is shy and has never previously met him, he should place his hand between her thighs, which she closes instinctively.

If she is very young he should place his hands on her breasts, which she will doubtless cover with her own hands, under the armpits and on the neck.

If she is a mature woman he should do everything which might please both of them and which is suitable for the occasion.

Then he should take her hair and her chin between his fingers to kiss them.

If the woman is very young she will blush and close her eyes.

By the way she responds to his caresses he can judge what pleases her most in love-making.

On this point, Souvarnanabha says: "Whatever man does for his own pleasure during intercourse, he should always press the part of the woman's body towards which she turns her eyes."

Here are some of the signs of enjoyment and satisfaction shown by a woman:

Her body relaxes, her eyes close, she loses all her timidity, and tries to ensure that the two organs are united as closely as possible.

On the other hand when she experiences no pleasure at all, she beats the bed with her hands, refuses to allow the man to advance; she is sulky, bites and kicks the man and continues to move her body even after the man has finished.

In such cases the man must rub the yoni with his hand and fingers (just as the elephant rubs with his trunk) before engaging in intercourse, until it is moist; only then should he insert his linga.

He resumes the same motion with his hand after his orgasm if the woman has not yet reached hers.

There are nine acts which the man must perform.

'Penetration' or *'forward motion'*. The two organs are brought towards each other directly.

'Churning'. The linga, held in the hand, is turned round and round in the yoni, around its edges (as one churns butter).

'Piercing'. The yoni is lowered and the linga strikes its upper part.

'Rubbing'. In the same situation the linga strikes the lower part of the yoni.

'Pressing'. The linga presses the yoni for a long time.

'The blow'. The linga is withdrawn from the yoni and then driven in deep and hard; such removal restores vigor to the linga, delaying the male orgasm; the rapid return tends to accelerate that of the female.

'The blow of the boar'. The linga, on re-insertion, strikes only one part of the yoni.

'The blow of the bull'. As it enters, the linga strikes both sides of the yoni at the same time.

'The sport of the sparrow'. Without leaving the yoni the linga is moved to and fro very fast.
This occurs rather late in the sexual act, when the man feels he can no longer delay his orgasm.

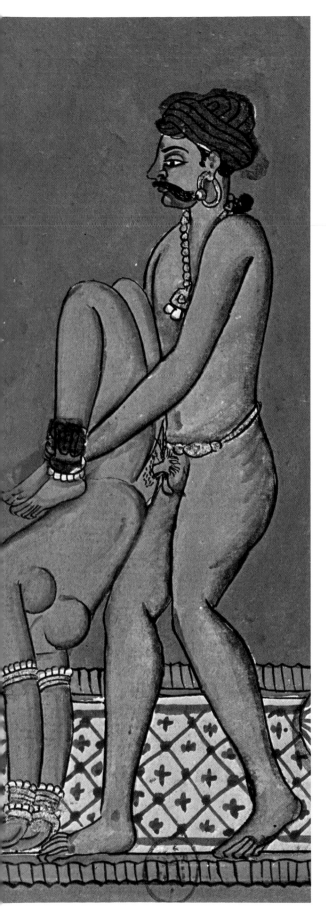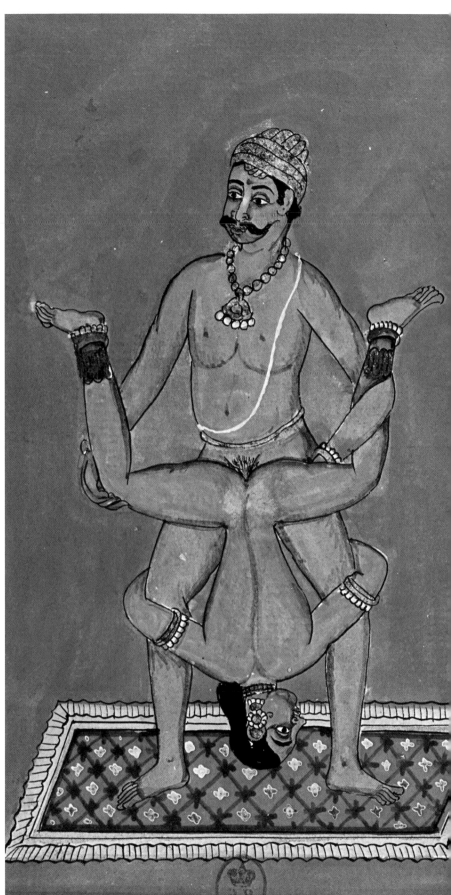

*"You were my conqueror—
now I, in turn, wish to make you
cry out for mercy."*

What happens when the woman takes the active role

When one of the lovers is in any of several physical conditions—particularly when the man is tired after fruitless efforts to produce an orgasm (some men can stay erect indefinitely in this way)—the woman may decide to take the active role. Sometimes, in so doing, she is influenced by the desire for change and by curiosity.

There are two situations: when the woman, during intercourse, pivots on top of the man so as to continue the sexual act without interrupting her pleasure; and when she takes the man's position from the very start.

In this latter instance, with flowers in her loose hair, her smiles mingled with sighs, she squeezes her breasts against her lover's chest, and, lowering her head repeatedly she caresses him in all the ways in which he used to caress her and excite her, saying to him: "You were my conqueror—now, I, in turn, wish to make you call out for mercy."

At intervals she will simulate shame, fatigue and the desire to end the sexual act.

However, besides the nine acts which belong properly to the man she should also perform the following three.

'*The pincers*'. She holds the linga in the yoni, draws it in by a sort of repeated suction, squeezes it and keeps it within her for a long time.

'*The pivot*'. During intercourse the woman turns around the man like a horizontal wheel turning around a vertical axis.

'*The balance*'. This is the opposite of 'churning'; the man raises the middle of his body and the woman imparts a turning and oscillating motion to her own middle parts and to the united organs.

When the woman is tired, she places her head on her lover's and stays in that position, without separating the organs. When she has rested, the man turns about her and resumes the act.

*"In respect of the practices of love,
one should be guided only by the customs of the region
and one's own taste."*

Auparishtaka, or oral intercourse

There are two sorts of eunuchs, those who dress up as men and those who seek to be taken for women.

Everything that is done to the female jagdana is done in the mouth of such eunuchs. It is called *auparishtaka*. This is how these eunuchs, who live like courtesans, make a living.

Eunuchs who dress up as men hide their desires. When they wish to indulge them they serve as professional masseurs.

A eunuch of this sort draws towards him the thighs of the man he is massaging and touches him on the joints of the thighs and the jagdana.

If he finds the linga erect he excites it with his hand.

If the man, thus apprised of his intentions, does not tell him to administer *auparishtaka*, he begins to set about it himself.

However, if the man actually asks him to do it, the eunuch pretends to be offended by such a proposition, and agrees to do it only with great reluctance.

He then performs eight graded exercises, proceeding from one to the next only when told to do so by the man.

'Nominal intercourse'. Holding the linga in his hand and squeezing it between his teeth, the eunuch moves his mouth.

'Biting on the sides'. The eunuch encloses the end of the linga in his tightly cupped hand, like the bud of a plant or a flower, and squeezes its sides with his lips and even with his teeth.

'External suction'. The eunuch presses the end of the linga with his tightly closed lips, ejecting it by means of such pressure and then re-inserting it with his lips, several times.

'Internal suction'. The eunuch inserts the linga into his mouth, squeezes it with his lips and withdraws it; he then puts it back into his mouth and continues as before.

'The kiss'. Holding the linga in his hand, the eunuch kisses it in the manner described for the kiss of the lower lip.

'Licking'. After the kiss, the eunuch touches the linga on all sides with his tongue and licks the end.

'Sucking a mango'. The eunuch puts half the linga inside his mouth and sucks it hard.

'Swallowing'. The eunuch inserts the entire linga into his mouth, pressing it in as far as it will go, as if he wished to swallow it.

58

Male servants sometimes perform *auparishtaka* on their masters. It is also practised among adults in private.

A number of woman of the harem, with particularly ardent sexual desires, also do it to each other, joining mouth and yoni (this is done in lesbian or Sapphic love: the titillation of the clitoris by the tongue).

Some men caress the yoni in this way, using the same type of love play as in the kiss on the mouth. In such cases, when the woman is turned over, head down, towards the man's feet, he caresses her yoni with his mouth and tongue. This is the 'mating of the crow' (illustrated in the underground temple of Elephanta).

Their passion for this kind of pleasure leads some women to abandon highly meritorious and generous lovers in order to go with slaves and elephant drivers.

In contrast with the opinions of the ancient casuists, who are more severe, Vatsyayana feels that *auparishtaka* is prohibited only between men and their wives. He adds that, in respect of the practices of love, one should be guided only by the customs of the region and one's own taste.

The *apadravyas,* or accessories

In order to satisfy a woman, a man may also use what are known as *apadravyas* —objects which, when placed on or around the linga, make it longer or thicker, so that it corresponds to the dimensions of the yoni.

Bathravia holds that these objects should be of gold, silver, copper, iron, ivory, buffalo horn, certain woods, leather or skin; they should be gentle and cool, induce erection and generally be appropriate for their purpose.

In this respect Vatsyayana leaves the decision to each individual.

Here are the various sorts of *apadravyas.*

'The armlet' *(valaya)* is the same length as the linga; its outer surface should be rough and covered with small globules, forming a soft but lasting file.

'The couple' is formed of two armlets.

'The bracelet' *(chudaka)* consists of several armlets the total length of which equals that of the linga.

'The spiral' is made by rolling around the linga a metallic thread, perhaps brass, very closely bound.

The *jalaka* is a metal tube open at both ends. Its outer surface is coarse and covered with hemispheric protuberances which are soft to the touch; it is the same size as the yoni and is attached to the belt.

If a *jalaka* is unobtainable one should use a tube made from the wood of the apple tree, or the tubular neck of the gourd, or reeds softened with oils and essences, attached by string to the belt; or a large number of small, soft wooden rings, attached together.

The tubes can be used either as a sheath around the linga, or instead of it.

In the south of India it is customary to make a hole in the skin of the linga, just as one would pierce one's ears in order to wear earrings. Several *apadravyas* may then be attached to this hole: those referred to above as well as others conducive to the pleasure of the woman.

The author tells how to enlarge the linga for a month by rubbing it with certain plants.

He claims that, in the Dravidian areas, a lasting enlargement can be assured by rubbing the linga with the silks of certain insects which live in the trees, like the caterpillars, and then, for two months, with oil, and then again with the silks of insects, and so on.

The linga gradually swells; when it is big enough, the man lies down on a hammock through which a hole has been made for him to let his linga hang; he then suppresses the pain of the swelling by means of cold lotions.

The aphrodisiacs

They are prepared as follows.

Put some Chaba pepper in sugared milk and then add to it: 1) a decoction of the uchala root, or seeds of *sanseviera*, or *roxburghiana*; 2) *hedysarum gangeticum,* or the sap of that plant with it; 3) the juice of the kuiti and the kshirika; or 4) a paste consisting of branched asparagus and the shvadaustra and goudachi plants, with the addition of honey and mistletoe (this latter plant is known to have been used in magic concoctions by the Druids); or 5) a decoction of the last two plants, with the fruits of the *premna spinosa*; 6) sugared milk in which goat testicles have been boiled; 7) a blend of honey, sugar and ghee, in equal proportions. Fennel juice in milk is a nutritious aphrodisiac which prolongs life and is drunk like nectar; 8) a multiple decoction, similar to the first five given above, whipped with sparrow's eggs (this being a highly amorous bird), makes a man capable of satisfying many women.

Another complicated recipe, containing only vegetables, enables a man to make love to an unlimited number of women.

The following aphorism sets forth the general rule on this subject:

The means of producing sexual vigor and passion must be taken from medicine, the Vedas, magic and discreet relatives.

One should never try any aphrodisiac which has dubious effects or may be harmful to the health, or any which involves the killing of an animal or any unclean contact.

Use should be made only of those which are healthy, which have been confirmed by experience and approved by the Brahmans.

64

*"She should try to conquer the heart
of a vigorous, good-looking young man."*

The young woman who conquers a husband

When a young woman endowed with fine qualities and a good education belongs to a family of lowly status, and therefore receives no attention from suitors of her caste; or when a young woman who observes the rules of her family and caste is an orphan with no relatives to look after her, she must take it upon herself, when the time comes, to find a husband.

She should try to conquer the heart of a vigorous, good-looking young man, or a man whose irresolute nature suggests to her that marriage is possible even without the consent of his parents.

She should use every possible means of captivating him, by seeing and talking to him frequently. Her mother should also use her friends and her foster-sister as a way of arranging frequent meetings, either at her friends' homes or elsewhere, with the coveted husband. For her part, the young woman should try to be alone with him, in some safe place where they will not be disturbed, and from time to time should offer him gifts of flowers, perfumes and betel nuts and leaves.

She should show him her talents in the arts of massaging, scratching and pressing with her nails; she should discuss with him things which he finds entertaining or interesting, including the ways and means of winning the heart of a young woman.

Ancient authors agree that the young woman, even if she is in love, should not make the first move; she should merely encourage her suitor, allow him some measure of intimacy, and receive the manifestations of his love without appearing to notice his passion.

When he tries to steal a kiss she should at first resist; when he asks for intercourse she should refuse; she should merely allow him to touch certain hidden parts, while at the same time making it difficult for him, and resist any attempts to go further.

Only when she is sure of his love and his constancy and he is determined to marry her promptly, should she consent to yield to him.

Once she has thus lost her virginity she can so inform her friends.

"Ganikapati thinks that there are circumstances which justify intercourse with other men's wives."

Cases in which love is permitted

When it is practised in marriage contracted in accordance with the rules outlined by Manu, between persons of the same caste, Kama produces legitimate offspring and general esteem.

It is prohibited with women of higher caste or with women of the same caste who have already belonged to other men.

Kama is neither prescribed nor prohibited with women of lower caste or women expelled from their caste, with courtesans and with divorced women.

With all these women the practice of Kama serves exclusively to provide pleasure.

Women with whom mating is possible without sin are known as Nayikas; these are young women who are dependent on no-one, courtesans and women who have been married twice.

Vatsyayana includes in these three categories widows, the daughters of courtesans, female servants who have not lost their virginity, and even those caste women who have exceeded the age of puberty without getting married.

Ganikapati thinks that there are circumstances which justifty intercourse with other men's wives. For example, the following reasoning may be applied, depending on the nature of the case:

"This women wishes to make love with me, and has already made love with numerous other men before me; although she is of higher caste, she is in circulation like a courtesan; so I can make love with her without sinning."

"I have an enemy who can do me great harm; if his wife becomes my mistress she will change his hostility towards me."

"With the help of this or that woman, if I am her lover, I will be able to guarantee the victory of my friend or the downfall of my enemy, or the success of some exceedingly difficult enterprise."

"I have no resources and no way of getting any, so intercourse with this or that woman will bring me wealth without risk."

"This or that woman loves me ardently and knows all my secrets, all my weaknesses and can, accordingly, do me great harm if I do not become her lover."

"A husband has seduced my wife, so I must get my own back." (The Law of Retaliation).

Seduction of a young woman with a view to marriage

First of all the suitor must win the young woman's foster-sister over to his cause; then he teaches her the sixty-four ways of sexual enjoyment used by men and boasts to her of his talents in this domain.

He is always well dressed and makes the right impression on those who see him; young women fall in love more easily with suitors who are good-looking and presentable.

A young woman always betrays her amorous feelings by certain signs or acts, such as the following. She never looks the man in the face and feels embarrassed and ashamed when he looks at her. On some pretext or other she shows him her limbs; she looks at him furtively when he goes away, lowers her head when he asks her a question, and answers him awkwardly, in incomplete sentences. She is happy to be in his company for long periods, and talks to his female attendants in a special tone so as to attract his attention when he is a certain distance away. She takes care not to leave the place where he is, devises pretexts for showing him certain objects and tells him long anecdotes, just so as to remain in his company a little longer. She kisses and embraces a child who might be sitting on his knees, makes graceful or amusing gestures when her maids-in-waiting speak to her in the presence of the man she so ardently desires, and she is particularly trusting and deferential towards his friends. She is kind to his servants, listens to them carefully, or talks to someone else about their master. Whenever her foster-sister or her friends happen to have arranged a visit to his house, she willingly goes to talk and play with him. She tries not to be seen by him in informal attire, and has a friend show him her earrings, jewelry and garlands which he has asked to see. She always wears things which he has given her, is terribly upset when her relatives even mention the name of some other suitor and flies into a rage at anyone who dares speak in support of a rival.

Here are some verses on this subject:

"A man who has, through external signs, recognized the feelings a young woman has for him must do everything necessary to be united with her. He will captivate a very young girl by childlike games, a young woman by his talents (in the Kama Sutra, no doubt), and a woman who is in love with him through go-betweens he trusts."

When the lover has won the heart of the young woman he completes the process of seduction by various means, such as these:

When he is with her, engaged in some game or exercise, he takes her hands meaningfully, and practises on her all the embraces described in the Kama Sutra.

Sometimes he shows her a figure cut in the leaf of a tree, depicting two lovers mating; he is visibly delighted at the sight of new buds of flowers and leaves, and the rising of the sap in spring.

He describes to her his torments, and tells her of a beautiful dream he has had about other women.

At gatherings of the caste he arranges to be near her; on some pretext he touches her, places his foot on hers; he gently and gradually touches her toes with his and presses them with the tip of his nails.

If he is not rejected he will then take her feet in his hand and clasp them delicately. He should also squeeze

one of her fingers between his toes; whenever he receives anything from her, or gives anything to her, he should, by his manner and look, convey to her the full extent of his love. When water is brought to him so that he may rinse his mouth, he should sprinkle it over her.

When he is with her in some isolated place he should caress her lovingly, conveying to her his passion, without upsetting or hurting her.

Whenever he is seated next to her on the same bench or bed, he should take her aside, explaining that he needs to talk to her privately; he should then express his love through gestures rather than words. He should take her hand and place it on his forehead; if she is visiting him he should keep her with him claiming that he is about to prepare a medication which would have no effect unless she also were to have a hand in making it.

When she leaves, he should urge her to come back; then, when she has become a regular visitor he should engage in long conversations with her, for, in the words of Gothakamouka, "no matter how much a man loves a woman, he will not win her unless he talks to her".

Lastly, when he sees that the young woman is completely subjugated he can begin to enjoy her.

If a young man is unable to achieve these results on his own, he should enlist the aid of the girl's foster-sister. She will persuade her to visit him — after which everything will go according to plan.

If there is no foster-sister he should send her one of his servants who could become friendly with her and work on his behalf.

He should see to it that he meets her at all public and private meetings, and when he is alone with her he can enjoy her. Because, as Vatsyayana says, "if the time and place are propitious, a woman will put up no resistance to the man she loves".

The honeymoon

When the feasting and ceremonies of marriage are over (after puberty), during the night of the tenth day, and not before, the husband may stay alone with his wife; he should speak to her tenderly, draw her to him and press her gently to his breast, to begin with in the manner preferred by the young woman herself, and on each occasion for only a few instants.

He will then proceed to touch her, starting with the upper part of the body, because it is simpler and easier.

If the young woman is timid and completely ignorant, and if he is still not familiar with her, he should try his first caresses in the dark. If she consents he will put in her mouth a *bambula* (betel nut and leaf); he will deploy his full eloquence to persuade her to accept it, if necessary even kneeling before her; this is because a woman, no matter how angry or timid, will never reject a man kneeling imploringly at her feet.

As he gives her the *bambula* he should kiss her gently on the mouth. Then he should get her to talk to him, by asking questions about things he professes not to know, and which she can explain in a few words. If she does not reply he will be patient, repeating his questions calmly, and encouraging her to reply; for, as Govakamoukka says: "Young women listen to everything men say, but without uttering a word."

By insisting, he will ensure that she replies, if only by nodding. When he asks her if she loves him or desires him, she will remain silent a long time; then, eventually, feeling herself under pressure, she will not assent.

A friends of hers, present for the occasion, might reply for her, and even have her say more than she intended; the young woman will scold her, smilingly, and cast a glance at her lover which indicates her acquiescence.

If the young woman is familiar with her husband she will place around his neck a garland of flowers, in response to his express wish; he will take advantage of this opportunity to touch her breasts and fondle them with his fingers. If she tries to stop him, he should say: "I will not start again, as long as you keep embracing me."

When she is in this position, he will place his hand several times on her neck and nearby parts of her body. From time to time, he will place it on her knees, press it to his bosom and seek her consent to intercourse. If she holds back he should threaten to make nail and teeth marks on her breasts and arms, and to make similar marks on his own body, and then to go about saying that she was the one who made them.

The next two nights, as the young woman yields to him more and more fully, he should caress her all over her body and cover her with kisses, placing his hands on her thighs and fondling them gently. From there he should pass to the groin; if she removes his hands, he should ask: "What's wrong with that?", and so persuade her to comply with his wishes.

Having obtained this favor, he should touch her sexual parts, undo her belt and the knot securing her lower garment; he should also massage the upper part of her naked thighs. All these things will be done on various

pretexts, but without actually engaging in intercourse. Then he should teach her the sixty-four ways of Kama, telling her of his love for her and of all that he expects from her. He should promise eternal fidelity and assure her that she will never have a rival.

Lastly, once he has overcome her shyness, he should consummate the union and enjoy her without frightening her.

By acting in this way, according to the inclinations of the woman, the man gains her love and trust.

Success is not achieved by absolute submission or by inflicting brutal violence on the woman's will; a man who is too easily influenced by a girl's refusal will be despised by her, as being ignorant of the hearts of women; yet a woman who has been enjoyed against her will is certain to hate the man who has shown such disrespect for her.

Obstacles to relations with the wives of other men

It is permitted to seduce the wife of another man, if one runs the risk of dying of love for her.

The intensity of this love has ten degrees related to the following effects:

1) love of the eyes; 2) attachment of the mind; 3) constant reflection; 4) loss of sleep; 5) loss of weight; 6) dislike for entertainment; 7) neglect of decency; 8) madness; 9) fainting; 10) death.

According to Vatsyayana it is possible to tell whether a young woman is passionate from her behavior, her conversation and the movements of her body.

As a general rule, says Gonikapoutra, a man's beauty always impresses a woman, and that of a woman always impresses a man; but more often than not various considerations prevent them from acting on this impression.

The attitudes of a woman in love are as follows:

She loves without worrying about what is right or wrong; she does not seek to conquer a man out of self-interest. When a man courts her, her first instinct is to reject him, even if she desires him. But she yields to repeated, insistent overtures.

On the other hand a man who is in love with a woman controls his passion, whether through scruples or reason; and even though he is unable to divert his thoughts from a certain woman, he resists when she tries to lead him on.

Sometimes a man abandons his campaign after one initial failure.

When he has eventually succeeded, he often becomes indifferent.

A woman may reject the advances of a man for the following reasons:

Devotion to her husband; fear of having illegitimate children; lack of suitable opportunity; hostility due to an excessively blunt declaration on his part; differences of rank; uncertainty about his having to be away traveling; fear that he loves another woman; the thought that his friends might mean everything to him; fear of indiscretion; shyness towards an extremely famous, powerful or clever man; fear about the ardor of his passions if she is a Gazelle Woman (yoni No. 1); the thought that she may have previously been friendly with him; contempt for his lack of wordly wisdom; disquiet about his bad reputation; resentment at his failure to understand her love for him.

If she is an Elephant Woman, the thought that he is a Hare Man, or cold; fear that her passion for him might have bad consequences for her; distrust of her own charms; fear of being discovered; disillusionment at the sight of his white hair or puny body; fear that he might have been secretly assigned by her husband to check on her fidelity; and the thought that he might be too severe.

78

Men who are successful with women

Men who are successful with women are the following:

Men well versed in the science of love; men gifted at telling stories; those who have lived since childhood in the company of women; those who know how to win their confidence; those who send them gifts; those who talk well; those who know how to satisfy their desires; those who have not yet had any other woman; men who act as messengers; those who know their weaknesses; men who are desired by decent women; those who are good-looking; those who have been raised with them; their neighbors; men who can devote themselves completely to sexual pleasures, even if they are servants; the lovers of foster-sisters; men who were until recently married and have since become widowers; those who are fond of parties and elegant society; generous men; those who are renowned for their strength (Bull Men); brave and enterprising men; men who are superior to their own husbands in knowledge, good looks, good qualities and generosity; men who dress and live magnificently.

Any man who is concerned for his reputation never tries to seduce a young woman who is fearful, timid, not to be trusted, or well guarded, or one who has a brother-in-law or a mother-in-law; abstention is recommended here for reasons of prudence, but not of morality or religion.

When a woman takes offense and rudely rejects a man who seeks her favor, he should abandon his efforts at once. On the other hand, if, while scolding him, she continues to be affectionate and gracious to him, he should spare no effort to win her love.

How to recognize a woman's feelings and inclinations

Whenever a man is trying to seduce a woman he must recognize her inclinations and act accordingly. If she listens to his flattery without showing in any way her own intentions, the man should seek the services of a go-between.

If, after a first meeting, she comes to a second more beautifully attired than before, or if she seeks out the suitor in some lonely place, he can be quite sure that she will put up only a weak resistance.

A woman who encourages a man but does not yield to him is a trickster in love; yet, because of the fickleness of the female mind, she may eventually give in, as long as the man maintains a very intimate friendship with her.

When a woman flees from a man's advances and, out of respect for him and for herself, avoids being in his company or coming near him, he may be able to seduce her, but only with great difficulty, either by striving for familiarity with her or by using a clever go-between.

When a woman meets a man alone and touches his foot, and then, through fear or indecisiveness, pretends that she did it by mistake, success can be achieved through patience and continual efforts, as follows.

If she happens to go to sleep near him the man should put his left arm around her and see if, when she wakes up, she rejects him sternly or in a manner which suggests that she wants him to start again. In the latter case he should embrace her more tightly. If she breaks away and stands up, but without changing her normal manner, he may conclude that she is anxious to surrender to him. If, on the other hand, she does not come back, he should send her a go-between. If she then returns, he may take it that she consents to be enjoyed by him.

When a woman offers a man an opportunity to demonstrate his love for her, he should enjoy her immediately.

Here are the signs whereby she may manifest her love:

She visits the house of the man she likes without being invited.

She arranges to be seen by him in isolated places.

When talking to him she trembles and is inarticulate.

Her fingers and toes are wet from sweat; her face becomes flushed with the pleasure of seeing him.

She takes pleasure in massaging his body and pressing his head.

When she massages him she uses only one hand, with the other, she touches and embraces the parts of his body.

She leaves her two hands placed motionless on his body, as if under the influence of surprise or fatigue.

She places one of the hands quietly on his body, and when he squeezes that hand between two of his limbs she leaves it there several minutes without withdrawing it.

Lastly, when she has resisted, for one whole day, all the man's attempts to seduce her, she comes back the next day to massage him as before.

When a woman, while neither encouraging nor avoiding a man, hides and remains alone, it is necessary to arrange for a serving girl to go and talk to her.

82

*"She should constantly seek
to increase her experience and her talents,
and she must always be seen to be liberal
and to enjoy pleasures and the arts."*

The proper motivation of courtesans

When a courtesan loves the man to whom she has yielded her body, her acts are natural; when, however, she has only money in mind, they are artificial and constrained. Even in this instance, she must still behave as if she were truly in love, since men trust women who appear to love them. While affirming her love she must give the impression that she stands to gain nothing; then, in order to avoid compromising her standing in men's eyes, she must refrain from taking money by unlawful means.

A courtesan must stand, nicely dressed, at the door of her house; and, without making herself too evident, she should look up and down the street so that she will be seen as an object on display in a shop window. She must be friendly with anyone who can help her win men away from other women and get rich, or protect her against insults or harassment. These are the guards of the town or the police, the agents and officers of the courts of justice; astrologers, powerful men and money-lenders; scholars, masters of the sixty-four liberal arts; jesters, jugglers, flower merchants, vendors of spirits, washermen, barbers and beggars; as well as anyone else who may be useful to her for any purpose.

Men whom she may take solely for their money are those who are lawfully in possession of their inheritance, young men, men who are free from all ties; civil servants, those who have assured incomes or means of support, men who pride themselves on their good looks; braggarts; eunuchs who conceal their true status; men who detest their equals; those who are naturally generous; those who are in good standing with the king and his ministers, men who always succeed in their enterprises, those who take pride in their wealth; brothers who disobey their elders, men on whom the members of their caste keep an eye; the only sons of rich fathers; ascetics tormented by the goad of the flesh; brave men; the doctor of the king; former acquaintances.

The courtesan may have relations with men endowed with excellent qualities, solely out of love or self-esteem, such as:

Men of noble birth, scholars, men with worldly wisdom and mature conduct; poets, entertaining storytellers, men endowed with eloquence or some particular artistic gift; farsighted men, men with great minds, persevering men and those with unswerving dedication; those who never get angry; those who are generous, affectionate towards their parents and who enjoy the pleasures of society; those who are skilled at completing verses begun by others, and at other intellectual pastimes; those who are in excellent health or who have great physical strength or perfection; those who never drink to excess, those who are powerful, sociable, fond of sex and having a captivating way with women, without allowing themselves to be dominated by them; those who know nothing of envy or jealous suspicions.

As for the courtesan, she should be beautiful and pleasant and have on her body certain auspicious signs. She should like good qualities in men, even while in pursuit of wealth. She should enjoy sexual relations emanating from love and should be, in such cases, of the same caste as the men to whom she yields her body. She should constantly seek to increase her experience and her talents, and she must always be seen to be liberal and to enjoy pleasures and the arts.

The author then lists the qualities which should be found in all women. They are those which could be expected of them in all countries, plus the knowledge of the Kama Sutra and the sixty-four talents which it teaches.

Next comes the list of the men whom the courtesan should avoid.

They are the same as anywhere else, plus: soothsayers; men who allow themselves to be bought, even by their own enemies; and, lastly, excessively shy men.

In the opinion of certain ancient casuists, the author adds, courtesans may give themselves away out of love, fear, vengeance, grief or resentment, curiosity, and for the sake of money, pleasure or the assiduity and constancy of relations, in order to make a friend or rid themselves of an importunate lover; because of *dharma* (religious merit), fame and a resemblance to a loved person; the constancy and poverty of a particular man or because he happens to live in the same place or has the same number as her for purposes of sexual intercourse, or, lastly, in the hope of getting rich quick.

Vatsyayana, however, feels that the sole motives of the courtesan should be: love, the desire to escape from poverty and the acquisition of wealth.

Money must be her principal objective and she should never sacrifice it for love. However, in cases of fear or difficulties of one sort or another, she should take account of strength and other qualities.

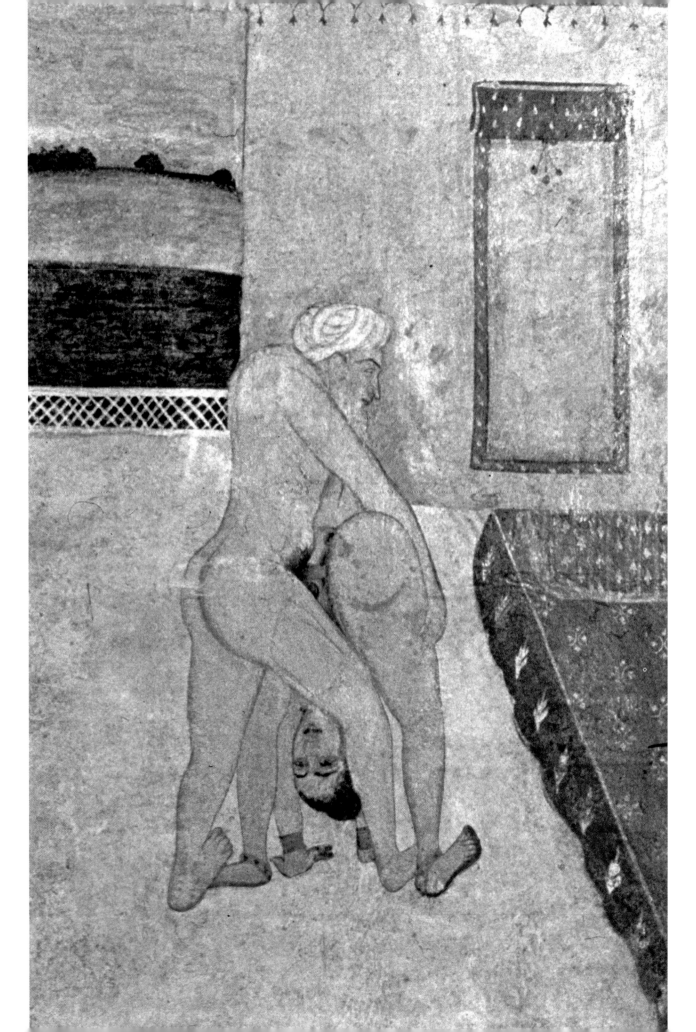

Ways of ridding oneself of a lover

Ridiculing and criticizing his habits and faults, while laughing in his face and stamping one's foot.

Talking about subjects he knows nothing about, belittling his knowledge, crushing his self-esteem, and seeking out the company of men superior to him in learning and intelligence.

Showing him contempt at all times, and criticizing men who have the same defects.

Dismissing as inadequate his efforts to arouse sexual pleasure; avoiding giving him one's mouth to kiss or allowing him to touch one's jagdana; showing contempt for the bites and scratches which he has administered to one's body, remaining limp in response to his embraces; lying absolutely still during intercourse.

Asking him to engage in sex when he is tired.

Making fun of his loyalty.

Refraining from returning his embraces, and turning away when he begins to make them.

Wanting to sleep or to go out to some appointment or other whenever he wants to have sexual relations during the day.

Parodying his words or gestures.

Laughing when he has not made a joke, or, when he has made a joke, laughing at something else.

Casting sidelong glances at one's own servants and twisting one's hands each time he opens his mouth.

Interrupting him in the middle of what he is saying and starting to talk about something else.

Listing his vices and flaws, while declaring them to be incurable.

Making offensive remarks about him to his servants, in his company.

Pretending not to notice him as he approaches.

Asking him to do things of which he is not capable.

And, lastly, dismissing him.

There is an aphorism about the proper conduct for a courtesan:

"The professional duty of a courtesan is, after a thorough examination and profound thought, to associate with a man endowed with what she wants; then to attach herself to the man with whom she is living, to get what she can out of him, and, finally, when she has taken everything, to send him packing. A courtesan who lives in this way like a married woman becomes rich without being exhausted by the number of her lovers."

Duties of an older wife towards the younger wives of her husband

During the lifetime of his first wife a man any take other wives, for the following reasons :

Madness or foul temper on the part of the wife, her husband's aversion towards her, sterility, failure to produce sons, incontinence of the wife.

When the woman is sterile or has no son, she should take it upon herself to persuade her husband to find another woman, give that woman a higher rank than her own, regard her as a sister, offer her sound advice, treat her children as if they were her own, and behave likewise towards her servants, friends and relatives.

If there are several women the oldest one should form a alliance with the one immediately after her in age and rank and should try to stir up trouble between the current favorite and the women who has been replaced by her in the master's esteem; then, having united all the wives against the favorite, she´ should openly side with the abandoned one and, without compromising herself in any way, she should have the favorite denounced as a spiteful, quarrelsome person.

If the favorite does quarrel with the husband, the first wife should feign sympathy for her, encouraging her to press her grievances and heightening her feelings of resentment. But if, despite all her efforts, the husband continues to love the favorite, she should switch tactics and work to reconcile them so as to avoid falling from favor herself.

*"Openly paying him lengthy business visits,
ensuring that one thing
will lead to another."*

3. The man should fondle a child who may be seated on her lap, giving it something to play with and then taking it away again so as to have a chance to talk to her and win the favor of her family. He should then proceed, after such a beginning, to visit the house regularly, taking care, during each visit, to talk about love when she is within earshot, even if she is not in the same room.

He should deposit with her some object or pledge, part of which can be taken back from time to time; he should also give her some perfumes or betel nuts to keep for him. The suitor should then establish a relationship between her and his own wife, so that they will have confidential and private conversations. In order to increase the frequency of their meetings he might arrange for the two families to have the same goldsmith, the same basket-maker, the same dyer and the same washerman. He will begin openly paying her lengthy business visits, ensuring that one thing will lead to another.

Whenever she needs anything, including money, or a knowledge of the sixty-four arts, he should point out to her that he is capable of doing all that she wants and of showing her everything that might please her. Similarly, he should hold discussions with her in the company of other people and they should talk about the remarks and actions of others, as well as subjects like jewelry and precious stones. In this case he should show her certain objects whose value she cannot possibly know, and, if she challenges his opinion of their worth, agree with her on all points.

This is the way to achieve intimacy with a woman.

"The woman becomes angry,
starts shouting, undoes her hair
and lets it fall loosely over her shoulders."

Go-betweens for amorous intrigues

Charayana says that it is permissible to associate with persons of lower status in order to secure their help in affairs of the heart: laundrymen, barbers, cattle drivers, florists, druggists, innkeepers, betel merchants, pithamardas (schoolmasters) and vidashkas (jesters).

A man may also be friendly with the wives of such people.

Go-betweens who are necessary for amorous intrigues should have the following qualities: skill, boldness, penetration, lack of scruples and shame, keen powers of observation and the ability to form an accurate assessment of all that is said, done or intended.

Good manners, a knowledge of the right time and place for any endeavor, sharp intelligence, swift judgment and resourcefulness in coping with emergencies.

There are several kinds of go-betweens or messengers of love:

1. *The go-between who does everything* is one who, having noticed the mutual love of two people, spontaneously sets about bringing them together.

2. *The go-between acting on her own account* is a woman who looks for a man to seduce or one who, while entrusted with an amorous intrigue, works for herself.

3. The married woman who works for her husband.

4. *The go-between who merely carries a letter;* she also brings the reply, which is usually oral.

5. When the love letter — like the reply — is hidden inside a bunch of flowers, the messenger if said to be 'mute'.

6. *The go-between who acts the part of the wind* is one who carries a message with two meanings, the real one of which is intelligible only to the person to whom it is addressed: the reply may be conveyed in the same way.

Female astrologers or fortune-tellers, beggars, servants or maids are clever go-betweens who quickly win the trust of women.

They know how to sow discord, when necessary, and how to praise a woman's charms and her talents in the art of love.

They are not bashful when circumstances require them to speak openly of a man's love, his sexual prowess and of the women — even more beautiful than the one he is wooing — who would be happy to have him as their lover; she explains how his family situation interferes with his efforts.

Lastly, a go-between can, by well chosen words, give a man a woman who has not even thought of him or who would seem to him to be well beyond his aspirations.

She is also able to bring back a lover who has chosen to become separated for some reason or other.

Cases in which love is forbidden

The school of Babhravya maintains that it is permissible to enjoy any woman who has had five lovers; but Ganakiputra thinks that, even in such a case, exceptions must be made for the wives of relatives, of a Brahman and of the king. Vatsyayana says that few women can resist a well-assisted man.

It is forbidden to have intercourse with the women listed below:

Lepers, lunatics, outcasts, those unable to keep secrets, those who publicly proclaim their carnal desires, albinos (there are impure) and those whose skin, which is intensely black, smells bad.

Women friends, women relatives, and ascetic women with whom intercourse is prohibited.

The following are regarded as women friends with whom intercourse is prohibited:

Those with whom we have played in the dust (childhood friends), to whom we are beholden for services rendered.

Those who have our tastes and temperament.

Those who have been our fellow-students.

Those who know our secrets and our shortcomings, as we know theirs.

Our foster-sisters and girls who were raised with us: hereditary friends, that is to say, girls from families united to ours by hereditary friendship.

These women friends must have the following qualities: sincerity, constancy, dedication, firmness, freedom from covetousness, incorruptibility, steadfast fidelity in keeping our secrets.

Relations between the king and his wives

The king's wives live lives of idleness, luxury and entertainment: they are never given anything tiring to do.

They attend festivals, concerts and shows, where they are treated with honor and are offered refreshments.

They are not allowed to go out alone; only women known to the guards and attendants are admitted into the harem.

Each morning the women who serve the women of the harem bring gifts of flowers, lily-of-the-valley and clothes from the king's wives to the king. The king then offers these gifts to the women, as well as similar objects worn by him the day before.

In the afternoon the king, clad in his full regalia, visits his wives, who are also ornately dressed to receive him. He shows them every sign of respect and assigns them to their places; then he holds a gay conversation with them.

Next he visits the remarried virgin widows, the concubines and the *bayaders,* each in her room.

When the king has finished his midday rest, the lady-in-waiting whose job it is to name the wife with whom he is to spend the night comes to him, accompanied by the maids of the wife whose turn has come and of those whose turn may have been missed inadvertently or through illness.

These members of the royal retinue present the king with essences and perfumes sent by their mistresses and marked with the seal of their ring, and explain to him the purpose of the gifts.

The king accepts the gift of one of them, who is thus notified of his choice.

Some kings, whether through scruples or compassion, take aphrodisiacs, so that they can serve several wives on the same night. Others, however, mate only with those they prefer, and neglect the others. Most kings give each of their wives a turn.

In conclusion

Once a man has made the acquaintance of a woman, if she betrays her love by various external signs and by the motions of her body, the man will go all the way; however, with a virgin, he should be delicate and careful.

When he has overcome her timidity he should exchange gifts, clothes, rings and flowers with her; these presents must be beautiful and costly. He should ask her to wear in her hair or carry in her hand the flowers which he had given her. Then he should take her aside, and kiss and embrace her. Finally, just as he is exchanging betel and flowers with her, he should touch and press her yoni, and, after duly exciting it, should complete the seduction.

When courting one woman, one should not, at the same time, try to seduce another. But when one has succeeded with the first and enjoyed her for a fairly long time, one can keep her affection by offering her gifts likely to satisfy her, and then embark upon another conquest.

When one sees that her husband has gone somewhere not very far from the house, one should do nothing to the woman, even if it is easy to win her consent.

To sum up, therefore, the man should arrange to be allowed into the woman's house and engage her in conversation. He should declare his love by insinuation, and, if she encourages him, should promptly begin a full-scale siege.

A woman who, at the first meeting, shows her love by external signs, can be had very easily. In the same way, a woman who appears delighted as soon as she hears a suitor's remarks may be regarded as virtually won. Generally speaking when a woman—whether wise, naive or trusting—does nothing to conceal her love, she has already capitulated.

Here are a number of aphorisms on this point:

"Desire which is born of nature, enhanced by art and protected by prudence, acquires strength and security. A clever and resourceful man will carefully note the thoughts and feelings of women and avoid anything which might hurt or displease them; in this way he usually succeeds with them."

A clever man who has learnt through the Shastras the ways of conquering the wives of others is never himself a deceived husband.

However, these methods should not be used for the seduction of married women, because they do not always work, and they expose one to cruel mishaps and to the loss of *dharma* and *artha*.

The art of seduction has been described here for the good of all, and to teach husbands how to keep their wives: they must not be used solely to seduce the wives of other men.

The linga and the yoni,
male and female sex symbols,
are revered throughout India.

How to make the acquaintance of a woman one desires

This is how a man can become united with the woman he loves:

1. The man should arrange to be seen by her, either by going to her house or by extending hospitality to her; or by meeting her at the house of a friend, a member of the same caste, a doctor or a minister, or also at weddings, sacrifices, parties, funerals and outings in the public gardens.

2. At each meeting the man should look at her so as to convey to her the full extent of his emotion: pulling on his moustache, biting his lower lip or making noise with his nails or ornaments he might be wearing, and other signs may serve this purpose. When the woman looks at him, he should speak favorably of her in the presence of her friends, comparing her to other women, and manifesting generosity and a love of pleasure. When seated next to another woman in her presence, he should feign boredom, distraction, fatigue and indifference to that other woman's remarks; he can also engage in a conversation, with a child or a grown woman, which is laden with innuendo and dual meanings, so as to convey his true feelings to her while pretending to talk about someone quite different.

The man can trace on the ground, with either fingers or a stick, figures which are related to her in some way. In her presence, he might embrace a child or give it, on his tongue, a mixture of betel leaves and nuts, while stroking the child's chin with his hand. All of these things should be done at the right time and in the right place.

94